WITHDRAWN

T M

THE LAST YEAR OF

THOMAS MANN

a revealing memoir by his

daughter, ERIKA MANN

translated by Richard Graves

Biography Index Reprint Series

 BOOKS FOR LIBRARIES PRESS
FREEPORT, NEW YORK

Translated from the German
Das Letzter Jahr

Photo credits:
frontispiece, Photo Caskey
photograph facing page 112, Thea Goldmann

INTERNATIONAL STANDARD BOOK NUMBER:
0-8369-8029-8

LIBRARY OF CONGRESS CATALOG CARD NUMBER:
72-126323

PRINTED IN THE UNITED STATES OF AMERICA

T M

I wish to talk about him—just that—about him, his plans, the story of his last year, the record of his last days and hours.

Once, when we were still living in California, he said to me, "When one is old and due to die, there is so much that oppresses one. A great cloud of anxiety and melancholy overshadows my latter days."

That is what he said once, but latterly—and I can say this with confidence—the cloud of apprehension dissolved and lightened as the evening mist dissolves when the sky and the night have made friends. No longer did we hear him quote Prospero's dreadful words: "And my ending is despair," which used to pierce his heart when he thought of his own ending.

Death was gentle with him, and the last year of his life was illumined and warmed by grace —the same that filled his "Joseph," that crowns "The Holy Sinner," and that was at last vouchsafed to him because he was true and had fulfilled himself. This grace was visible. Anyone who saw him toward the end of his life, whether in Stuttgart or in Weimar, in Lübeck, Kilchberg, or Zürich, in Amsterdam or The Hague, must have perceived the radiance that issued from him and illumined all his endeavors. He was, as is known, an accomplished speaker, a performer of the highest rank. Yet it is neither his talent nor his technique, nor the sum of both, that can explain the rare emotional force that emanated from him, especially toward the end. What touched and almost invariably captivated his audience was his personality, with all its secrets, its heights, and its

depths, which, when one thinks of them in con-
nection with a man of eighty, can only be called
the hallmarks of grace.

His last year—a year of grace and harvesting
despite resolute hard work and endless weari-
ness and anxiety—began in August, 1954, in
the Engadine. We had once more taken up our
quarters in the Waldhaus at Sils Maria and
there had met the Hesses, the German novelist
and his family, who were staying, according to
their custom, in the hotel. In previous years,
when we had been accustomed to come over at
irregular intervals from California, we had seen
more of the Hesse family than since our "home-
coming" to Switzerland. Montagnola, where
the Hesses lived, had always been an indispen-
sable port of call in our European journeys, and
we had passed countless hours in Hermann
Hesse's stronghold above the Lake of Lugano.
Now, in any event, we were living in Switzerland, and the fact that we were neighbors had
to compensate us for many an actual meeting.

Thus our summer reunion at the Waldhaus
during "the holidays," as the Swiss say, was all
the more enjoyable. My father loved the expression "holidays," which lent to his days of re-

laxation and recreation a perfume from the dreamlike loveliness of the real holidays of his boyhood, and brought to his mind the memory of the bight of Travemünde in his own home waters.

In point of fact, since he had been a writer, T.M. had never had any real holidays. His work was suspended only during his lecture tours or when he was ill in bed with a temperature, and now in Sils, as at home, it was his work that dictated the program of the day.

The galley proofs of "Krull" kept arriving, and it took time to correct them; however, the early hours of the forenoon were dedicated to the principal work on which T.M. was busy, in this case the essay on Chekhov. When this was completed, my father read it aloud to us, sitting in his beautiful corner room opening on the balcony, looking sheer down onto La Chasté and upward to the Fextal. Who would have guessed that T.M. would have devoted so much time and labor to the study of Anton Chekhov, the Russian master of the short story, the creator of "Uncle Vanya" and "The Sea Gull"? But the pages of my father's essay, while revealing a natural sympathy for the Russian, tell almost as much about the essayist as about the subject of his study.

Toward the end, we read, "I wish to declare that I have written these lines with deep sympathy, conquered by the poetry of my theme. Chekhov's ironical attitude to fame, the doubts he felt regarding the sense and value of his work, his disbelief in his own powers, contain in themselves the elements of quiet, modest greatness. 'Dissatisfaction with oneself,' he said, 'is one of the foundation stones of every real talent.' Here his very modesty becomes self-affirmative. 'Rejoice in your discontent,' he means to say; 'it is the proof that you surpass the self-satisfied and it may even show you to be great.' But he insists without compromise on the necessity for sincere doubt and self-dissatisfaction, and for him work, pursued relentlessly to the end with the consciousness that one knows no answers to the final questions, while one's conscience pricks one for throwing dust in the eyes of one's readers, remains a strange obligation in spite of all."

Unexpectedly, the pronoun "he," which had referred to Chekhov, becomes "one," and if this "one" is not finally changed to "I," the repersonification is defective only grammatically; in essence it is complete.

"It comes to this," concluded my father. "One delights a forlorn world with one's stories without ever being able to offer it a trace of saving truth. Poor Katya, in 'A Tedious Tale' asks 'What am I to do?' And what is the answer? 'On my honor and conscience, I don't know.' But still one goes on working, tells stories, gives form to truth and thereby delights a hungry world, hoping darkly, sometimes almost confidently, that truth and gracious form will avail to set free the human spirit and prepare mankind for a better, lovelier, worthier life."

Somewhat later, in the early spring of 1955, T.M. gave a public reading of his essay on Chekhov to the Zürich Authors' Society. I have before me the text that he read, with the cuts marked in red ink and a few underlinings, one of which emphasizes the word "almost" in the last sentence—"almost confidently." It was a sign of the grace that possessed him in his latter days that he could dispense with the "almost." Instead of underlining it, he might have replaced it by a frank affirmative.

The essay on Chekhov, onto which, unanticipated by us, T.M. had grafted so many self-revealing passages, touched us very deeply, though as he read it, my father did not betray his own emotion. I recollect only three occasions on which his voice faltered during his family rehearsal of public talks: in reading the description of the sufferings and death of the child Echo in "Faustus;" in the speech he made for my mother's seventieth birthday; and, finally, when rehearsing his tribute to Friedrich Schiller, his last great literary effort, on which he started to work as soon as he had finished his study of Chekhov.

My father felt well in Sils. He had recovered so completely from the lung operation of which, nine years before, he had nearly died, that he could stand the altitude—1,800 metres —without inconvenience, and was able to venture on considerable walking expeditions to his favorite beauty spots with my mother, his constant companion.

When my parents were out, I used to lie and write on my father's balcony, where, at other times, I did not wish to disturb him. I used to hear them going out and coming in, always conversing cheerfully, like two old friends with much to say to each other after a long absence. But they were always like that. During their life together of over fifty years, they were never for a moment bored with each other's company.

In the dining room in the Waldhaus, Hesse and his wife sat not far from us, it being tacitly understood that the two families should take their meals apart. It was only after dinner that they joined us. Looking back on those hours of talk, it seems to me that though serious subjects were, of course, often discussed, the general color of the conversation was gay and contemplative. Hesse laughs readily, and with his unhurried countryman's speech and circumstantial, appropriate gestures he can be extremely funny. No one appreciated him more than my father. T.M. also took his part in storytelling, reviving memories of his school days as he husbanded the long ash of his cigar and Hesse sent for another quarter of the local red wine.

Easy-mannered, talkative, companionable, and courteous, too, is how I would describe Hesse, the Lone Wolf (*Steppenwolf*), whose shyness and desire for solitude vanishes whenever he finds himself sitting with friends around a table. And my father and Hesse were true friends, brothers in spirit, who never let anything come between them and who put up a strong resistance when anyone tried to play off the one against the other.

Toward the end of our stay at Sils, the weather broke. Rainstorms lashed the lake and snow began to fall higher up the mountain. The pass was deep in snow and the road blocked. We wintered for a few days in the Waldhaus, until, with a return of sunny autumn days, we were able to drive along the old familiar stretch of road over the Julier and down to Tiefencastel, then up to Lenzerheide, sheer down to Chur, and once more steeply upward to the Kerenzerberg. I drove with my father sitting beside me and, as always on our journeys by car, with my mother ensconced in the narrow corner left free by our piled-up luggage. My father enjoyed motoring—he preferred it to any other form of travel—and the feeling of comfortable privacy that possessed him as soon as the car was in motion transferred itself to his chauffeur, in whom he had a childlike confidence.

It was for the last time: Sils, the Hesses, the drive through his beloved mountains, the ever-fresh astonishment mingled with a tinge of fear at the moon-craterlike aspect of the scenery at the top of the pass, the halt at Lenzerheide—all this for the last time. We could not foresee it then; there was no sign of coming disaster—not even a hint.

That autumn, "Krull" came out, and for the first time T.M. showed an inner concern about the reception of one of his books. He felt that the book ought to give people pleasure, to entertain them and make them laugh. Only then would he wish to go on with the story. Otherwise, the projected volume of "Memoirs, Part I," would remain a fragment.

And, indeed, it remains a fragment, though the success of the initial book had nothing to do with that, for, in fact, it sold more quickly than any of his previous works. If, nevertheless, and in spite of the grateful pleasure with which T.M. followed the success of his "Felix," not a line of the sequel was ever written, the fault is to be ascribed to the priority he gave a program of work he sketched out for me in a letter dated June 7, 1954, which ran as follows: "I have got an idea of doing a gallery of characters from the Reformation period. Lightning sketches of

Luther, Hutten, Erasmus, Charles V, Leo X, Zwingli, Münzer, Tilman Riemenschneider, and emphasizing the almost comic contrasts between the vastly different attitudes, viewpoints, and destinies of these figures as set against their common historical background."

He soon dismissed the notion of the gallery in favor of a theatre piece, in which he proposed to use a few short scenes from Reformation history. The play would center around Luther's wedding, a theme that Wagner had once thought of using as a plot for an opera instead of "Die Meistersinger." My father was busy on this project till the end.

He had loved the theatre all his life, and had always cherished the hope of one day writing a play more suitable to the needs of the stage than "Fiorenza," which dates from his thirtieth year. Since then, his interest in the theatre had been intense and constant. He had made a careful and accurate study of the activities of everyone connected with it, from the stagehands to the directors, and also, most important of all, the dramatist. He was determined to find out sooner or later how to construct a faultless piece. Shaw he thought particularly helpful as a model. During his last holidays, in Noordwijk, he had taken several volumes of the collected edition of G.B.S.'s plays with him and had read them, in the much abused translation of Siegfried Trebitsch, with real pleasure.

After their return from Sils, my parents stayed only a week at home. Then came their journey to the Rhineland, their first since the Nazis came to power.

In Cologne, the University was holding its international summer school, to which T.M. offered some plums from "Krull" in a reading, at the end of which he took part in a discussion with the students during the question period. He gave another talk on this subject in Düsseldorf. A number of photos taken to illustrate this journey were collected in two handsome albums and presented to my father. Looking through them, one seems to be watching a film, so lively and direct is the personality of the hero, who never for a moment looks like a sick man.

The study of Chekhov was preceded by an essay on Heinrich von Kleist. My father had written about Kleist in a preface to a volume of collected stories designed to introduce that author to the American public, and in the late autumn of 1954 he lectured on him to the students of the Technical High School at Zürich.

The lecture evoked storms of enthusiasm, owing not so much to the speaker's careful literary handling of a difficult subject as to its intrinsic merit as a lecture, for as a lecturer no one could compete with T.M.'s matchless artistry. The reception accorded this talk was an unusual phenomenon and deserves to be placed on record. A writer full of years who was not offering neat and complete specimens of ecstatic lyric poetry but only bare fragments of stubbornly personal prose—who would have thought that such a performance could arouse so much enthusiasm!

My father continued to work at his essay on Schiller, though it would be juster to refer to his activity at this period as preparatory to the real business of composition. In any case, it was long before he had come to the end of his preliminary studies. He read, made excerpts, and immersed himself with consuming passion not only in all that Schiller had ever written, experienced, and planned but also in everything related to or associated with the subject. In the end, he had acquired material sufficient for several books on Schiller. The text of his study, which he composed under difficulties rare in his experience, grew into a script covering no less than a hundred and twenty typescript pages, instead of the twenty-two that was to be the maximum length for his lecture.

Schiller was very near to my father and always had been. So familiar was T.M. with Schiller and his writings that it would have given him no trouble to speak extempore on any separate work of his, and I can imagine with what interest an audience at Stuttgart or Weimar or elsewhere would have listened to him. But this he did not, and could not, wish to do. This time, it had to be the whole of Schiller. If it was not possible to include every aspect of the man, the artist, his life, and his work within the compass of a limited study, it was nevertheless necessary to portray through the written, and spoken, word a living, breathing figure. No personal quality, no refraction of light in the halo to which new brilliance was now to be added, no feature in this nobly proud but unspeakably touching countenance must be forgotten.

Months passed. As though he felt this to be his final great effort, T.M. struggled with the overabundance of his material. "Ah," he sighed from the depths of his heart, "work is such an anxiety!" If anyone reminded him that every work he had embarked on had been an anxiety to him and that nonetheless he had been able to complete them all, he would say, "Yes, but this is exceptionally difficult, although"—he would add with a gentle smile, as if making excuses for himself—"work is my only joy." And, in truth, though work was not his only joy, without it he could not have taken pleasure in anything else. The fact of working and the feeling that he was making progress and was raising the quality of his writing to that of his conception were what made it possible for him to enjoy all he did enjoy. With that proviso, he was the most responsive of men. Music, the theatre, the beauty of men and things, a fine day, a child, an attractive animal—from all these he drew much pleasure, provided he was getting on with his work. Without work—that is, without active hope—he would not have known how to live. A life in which failing strength caused his achievement to fall short of his standards would have plunged him into the most terrible abyss of depression. Yes, indeed, he was able to give life to Peeperkorn's* deadly fear of emotional paralysis because he was haunted by a similar dread—the artist's fear that his creative powers are going to fail him. Peeperkorn says, "We have an obligation, a religious obligation, to feel things. Our feeling, you understand, is the manhood that brings life to being. Life without feeling is a slumber. It needs to be awakened to partake of a passionate union with the spirit of God. Man is nothing but the organ through which God consummates his marriage with the seething, raging ocean of life. If feeling is lacking, God is shamed and his manhood defeated and creation suffers a cosmic catastrophe, a horror beyond description."

Very well: this is a manner of thought and expression befitting the forceful figure in the book—the personality with the honor complex —but not befitting his creator. That the creative artist had the obligation, the religious obligation, to quicken sleeping matter with life, to give it a soul and a living form, was a positive article of faith with T.M. And though he was

* A character in *The Magic Mountain*.

not, of course, the sort of man to fill his mouth with words like "God is shamed" or "cosmic catastrophe" in talking of art, least of all his own, any failure of his creative manhood before his duty to give life to matter, and to shape and raise into the light that which lies formless in the dark, would certainly have filled him with unspeakable horror.

His study of Schiller was completed about Christmastime. "Friedrich Schiller in Love"—the title is characteristic of the essay, dedicated by irony to pathos, wherein, in his higher flights, the ironist refrains from every exercise of irony. The work of composition had exhausted him, and it was high time that something happened to restore him.

On January 16th, we left Zürich for Chur, this time by train, as the snow-covered mountain roads were not inviting to motorists. In Zürich, the sky had been overcast, but in Arosa the heaven was cloudless and the glittering snow fields flung the sunbeams back into the blue. The winter air was clear and scentless—purer still, it seemed, than that of the Engadine summer, with its tang of warm pine and larch needles. Could microbes, stimulators of disease, thrive here, bringing virus infections to a head —whatever one may understand from the purposely vague names the doctors give them? It may be so. The virus that attacked my father on the fourth night of our stay came inexplicably out of the pure air. Or, again, it may be that under an excess of hard work he had become susceptible to a poison he was carrying concealed in his body, and that the ozone of the high altitude, remedial as it is against germ-borne disease, may have shown itself, as in "The Magic Mountain," favorable to this particular virus. Anyhow, my father fell ill. It started with shivering fits, high fever, and bouts of nausea. Strong doses of antibiotics reduced his temperature within a few hours from 102.9 to below normal and his blood pressure from about 180 to 80. That was not good. The drops in temperature and pressure were too abrupt not to affect the heart and leave the patient in a state of exhaustion. "I feel disquietingly quiet," he said more than once.

Since our return from California, he had been repeatedly ill, and this was the second time that the holidays he valued so much had, seemingly, disagreed with him. In the spring just after finishing "Krull," he had had a vicious attack of influenza in Taormina, and now, immediately after completing the Schiller, he was confined to his bed among "those up here." Thinking it over, I came to the conclusion that the excitement he lived in while he was busy on an important work acted as a shield against the arrows of ill-health. But when he had written "finis" and had, without any express intention of so doing, entered a stage of relaxation, nature, overstrained, took her revenge and opened his defenses to poisons he was not accessible to in normal times. Only in the case of "Faustus" did this not happen; whether it was, as the author asserted, that the book itself had made him ill or whether he was already carrying the seeds of illness before he began to write, he found himself compelled, contrary to all precedents, to suspend his work on account of sickness. However, on that occasion his recovery, which surpassed in speed and completeness our—and the doctors'—most sanguine hopes, could only be attributed to the novel he had been forced to interrupt.

"The book," he writes in his essay on the origin of Dr. Faustus,* "was anchored in my heart. . . . Am I not right in thinking that my tractability as a patient, my almost unseemly talent for getting well quickly in spite of the handicap of age, my will to overcome, and to overcome easily, a late and unexpected physical affliction had a secret cause? Was it not to the service of this particular book that my subconscious self contributed a reserve of strength sufficient to enable me to go on and finish it?"

Often, as I sat by his bed at Arosa, I remembered these lines and asked myself, not without anxiety, how he would manage to extricate himself this time, when there was nothing anchored in his heart comparable in urgency with "Faustus." Of course, I was able to console myself with the thought that my father's illness was not to be mentioned for seriousness in the same breath with the grave visitation he had suffered in 1945 and that, moreover, sufficient purpose existed even now for him to fight the physical trials he might have to endure.

* "Die Entstehung des Doktor Faustus, Roman eines Romans," Bermann, Fischer Verlag, 1949 (not translated into English).

His heart held out well, and the clot we couldn't fail to be apprehensive about did not materialize. After a week, we were able to transport the patient by ambulance to the Cantonal Hospital at Chur. A scientific over-all checkup was carried out there, but apart from indicating a perfectly understandable but transient weakening of the organism, caused by illness, it brought no pathological symptom to light.

My mother, of course, was with him, while I stayed in Arosa. My presence might have made him think himself more seriously ill than he really was, and, furthermore, he was concerned about the work I was occupied with at the time and which I greatly needed to finish in an atmosphere of peace and concentration.

When he handed me his study of Schiller to be cut down, he said, "This time, I don't see how you can do it." I laughed and answered confidently, "I know how to deal with your things," and indeed I was not anxious about the successful outcome of my task. Given a small talent and a great love of the subject to be treated, one can say that in this modest field of work practice really does make perfect. And while I knew that by dint of my experience I was able to reduce T.M.'s essays by a third or even a half for platform purposes (though not to distill the whole thing to a fifth of its volume, as I had now to do), I had to make sure that the shortening of the text entailed a difference in volume only and not in essence. This time, my job did not involve reading over the essay a mere twenty times, as on previous occasions. I had to go through it fifty or sixty times; first in an entire reading, which was to eliminate passages superfluous in a lecture, and then in repeated study of the transitional form, by which new and at first unsuspected cuts were made feasible.

I telephoned to Kilchberg almost every day and reported to T.M. on the progress of my work, which I could not help describing as a kind of destructive torture, and received news of his progress toward recovery.

On February 11th, we celebrated my parents' golden wedding. As my father's eightieth birthday was in the offing, at which we proposed to assemble in full force, only Elizabeth (Medi) and Golo, of the children, apart from me, had made themselves free for this occasion. But,

most important of all, there was Nico, the black poodle, the woolly wedding gift we presented to the happy pair at breakfast, wearing a collar of Florentine gold leather with fringes of gold tinsel wherever they could be attached. Nico was the name of one of this dog's beloved and sagacious predecessors, which had been run over in America. For a long time past, "the Magician" had been thinking of a new Nico, and here he was. It was a complete surprise to T.M. when we carried Nico, sprawling, into the breakfast room, where the friendliest relations were soon established between "Master and Dog."

My father could now be considered cured except for some loss of weight, which he had not yet succeeded in making up. However, since his return home from Chur he had been able to resume his normal routine. He was busy on the episodes from Luther, which had come chiefly to dominate his working hours and continued to do so until the end. Forty-six octavo pages covered with small and closely written manuscript and containing an average of three hundred and forty words to the page bear witness to the progress my father had made with the project of Luther's marriage before he laid down his pen. The notes—excerpts, references, conjectures, conclusions, historical names, dates, and facts—are frequently underlined in red ink and, bearing witness as they do to the passionate industry of the prospector, give one a picture not so much of the planned work but, rather, of the encircling tactics by means of which (as in "Lotte in Weimar") the poet designed to fix and arrest the figure of his hero.

T.M.'s illness had caused his correspondence to fall into arrears, and much time was now spent in getting caught up with it. He also had to go for walks in his own interest and, more urgently, in Nico's, and the remainder of each day was devoted to minor literary work. During his last year, he wrote a large number of tributes, introductions, and pieces to commemorate various anniversaries. Finally, he had to compose an address in acknowledgment of the honor done to him when he was made a free citizen of Lübeck.

In the beginning of March, copies of the talk on Schiller—not yet the final version but an intermediate one of thirty-four pages—were dispatched to Theodor Heuss, President of the Republic at Bonn, and to the Schiller Society at Stuttgart. Professor Heuss had expressed the wish to be allowed to look at the manuscript as early as possible, so that he could avoid repetitions in his own speech. Meanwhile the Schiller Society had already begun to collect the contributions of all the collaborators, with a view to making a program covering the whole festival.

T.M. was in quite good form about this time. Although he contemplated finishing the Krull story one day, he felt himself free—for the moment, at least—from the heavy burdens he had so early accustomed himself to bear. As for "Luther's Wedding," he knew that it, too, was going to give him a great deal of hard work, but from the standpoint of length the play would have to be confined within certain limits, and he was consequently able to estimate the amount of effort it was likely to involve. In addition, he was still in the preparatory stage, in which almost everything capable of inclusion in a work or germane to its preparation seems too important, serviceable, and burningly interesting, as well as being sufficiently remote from realization in a text, for the author not to worry about the agonizing problem of deciding what to include and what to discard.

When I had reduced the Schiller to twenty-eight pages, I brought him the copy with my cuts.

"Finished?" he asked joyfully.

"Yes, I'm finished, but not the talk." And I explained that from now on no passage in the essay could be condensed any further without losing its function. A whole passage, six pages long, this one or that one, would have to be sacrificed in its entirety, and that would make it essential to compose a sentence or two leading to the text that followed. After luncheon, I kept my father company for a spell. Then came his siesta, as usual. Between tea and dinner, we dealt with no letters on this occasion, but seven whole pages of the Schiller fell victim to the author's red pencil, and I felt glad to be able to replace here and there a few sentences it had been a torture to delete.

Of course, T.M. was not happy about the Schiller address. When he reflected how much there was to say, and what, as he felt, was only hinted at in his talk, he found the result meagre, and was tormented by the fear that the audience would feel they were being cheated and getting short measure. Chekhov had never been able to rid himself of that fear when he thought of his readers. Nevertheless he had written, "Dissatisfaction with oneself is one of the foundation stones of every real talent." From my father's earliest days, this basic element of his talent had been operative, and the sincerity of his doubt in relation to his contribution to the Schiller Festival was no more open to question than in countless other like situations, one of which, dating from the dim past, provides a striking example of what I mean. My father had written a story called "Death in Venice." It was to appear in the *Neue Rundschau,* for which it had been commissioned. But when it was finished, T.M. refused to send it off. He had come to the conclusion that it was not good enough for the *Rundschau.* It was only my mother's affectionate protest that caused him to change his mind.

It should not be forgotten that he was naturally, unaffectedly, and even unconsciously a most modest man and that he often forgot what importance, for good or ill, was attached to his words by the general public.

"I have written to X," he said once, "and I haven't minced my words." We said that his letter should have been copied before it was sent off. X was a journalist, and might well publish the letter. The least one should have done was to keep a copy of the text to check against the published version in case of trouble. We were a bit shocked that T.M. had acted so incautiously. We wondered how this letter to X would look if weighed in the scales of public opinion. "No one," said my father confidently, "no one will bother about it. Practically no one reads the *Feldhuter Bote.*"

That was characteristic of my father. To the last, he seemed totally unaware that it did not matter from what platform he spoke or whether he had entrusted his prose to the columns of an obscure journal like the *Feldhuter Bote;* everything he said or wrote in certain contexts would be seized upon by the international news agencies and sparked around to all the capitals of the world. A hasty utterance, a wording open to misunderstanding, and other such improvisations were due to nothing but my father's optimistic modesty, which led him to believe, against all evidence to the contrary, that he could call himself Thomas Mann and yet provoke neither interest nor hostility if he wrote a letter to the *Feldhuter Bote* without mincing his words.

When, in the early spring of 1955, he was to read his essay on Chekhov to the Authors' Society of Zürich, the organizers of the meeting asked him to approve their choice of a large hall. However, my father remembered having been present at a talk given by a younger colleague of his for the same group in the salon of one of the Zürich hotels. He had been impressed by the comfortable and homely atmosphere on that occasion, and now wanted similar conditions for the evening of his own lecture. The delegates of the Authors' Society protested in vain. He could not be moved, with the result that not only were the lecture room and the adjoining salon, which had been made available for listeners, frightfully overcrowded but countless persons who had wished to hear the talk had to be turned away. The air was thick enough to cut with a knife, and the heat and the used-up atmosphere made it almost impossible to breathe. These trifles did not disturb the speaker. After a few moments of surprise and disappointment at the contrast between the conditions that evening and those that had prevailed at his colleague's lecture, he astonished his hearers by the untiring vigor and liveliness of his performance. It was not long since he had recovered from his illness at Arosa, and we feared that this might be too much for him. When it was all happily and safely over, my mother wanted to take "the Magician" home and give him a cup of his favorite chocolate before putting him to bed. What a hope! He spent two good hours chatting with colleagues downstairs in the hotel restaurant, and showed not the smallest sign of fatigue next day.

I have recorded this incident, which took place a few months before his eightieth birthday, not so much because it gives me an opportunity to praise his astonishing energy and productivity as because it bears witness to his natural modesty, which he combined with due self-respect and consciousness of his dignity as a man of letters and the obligations it entailed.

The deep anxiety with which he looked forward to the Schiller Festival was attributable to his natural modesty, as well as to the Chekhov-like dissatisfaction with his own talent. And he meant it in pure sincerity when, in the introductory part of his tribute to Schiller, he said, "Who am I to sing the poet's praise—I who see before my eyes mountains of skilled appreciation and discussion of his life and art, piled up during a century and a half of learned research." "Skilled appreciation" and "learned research"—these were phrases he used without a trace of mischief or coquetry. It was typical of him that he, so skilled in so many things and so deeply learned in so many fields, was always ready to bow before the professors. Every highly trained, specialized intellect could be sure of his ready appreciation, and not seldom he allowed himself to be overimpressed and even intimidated by intellectuality. "This is all so tremendously clever!" he would say as he put down the latest number of a hyperintellectual review containing an unpalatable concoction of sociology, music, and philosophy. "It is really frightening!" And he uttered these judgments seriously.

If I were to be asked what were the three most salient features in my father's portrait as an old man, I should not hesitate to name modesty, kindness, and humor. At the same time, I am fully conscious of the inseparability of the man and the artist, as well as being aware that without a great number of additional qualities neither the one nor the other comes to life. Nevertheless, though my summing-up seems oversimplified and thus not quite convincing, I cannot answer the question otherwise.

In regard to his humor, it is fair to say that none of his works is devoid of it. His gloomiest creation, Dr. Faustus, possesses it in fullest measure. All who knew "the Magician" well and were familiar with his gift for nonsense and absurdity and had seen him in tears of laughter over the comicalities of others, of which he could never have enough, must have realized what a leading part humor played in his life.

I have tried to give proof of his modesty by a number of instances, which could be multiplied indefinitely. I think I have said enough on this subject, and shall merely add that one can aim very high and remain very modest.

There are many who have experienced T.M.'s kindness in their own persons and many more who have become familiar with it through his writings. These will recall his express acknowledgment of this virtue in which he believed, although—or, rather, because—it need not be turned into a creed but can exist and function even as the product of doubt. This kindness of his illumined and warmed his art, whose principal concern was to diffuse "a little more of joy, gratitude, and divine cheerfulness among mankind."

He loved his fellow-creatures and deserved the tribute Hermann Hesse paid him in his funeral address. "In deep sorrow," he said, "I bid farewell to the dear friend and great colleague, the master of German prose, who despite all his honors and triumphs was misunderstood by many. The qualities that underlay his irony and his mastery of technique—his great heart, his loyalty, his sense of responsibility, and his capacity for affection—were for decades completely misinterpreted by the German public, but those are the qualities that will keep his work and his memory alive far beyond the span of our perplexed age."

And that is the truth. His love of mankind was loyal, and conscious of its responsibilities, and was inspired by a sense of solidarity. He says somewhere, "Does not all one's love for one's fellow-men rest upon compassionate, fraternal recognition of the almost hopeless difficulties of his life? Indeed this feeling should be the basis of a kind of human patriotism. One loves one's fellow-men, because their lot is hard and because one is oneself a man."

"Human patriotism!" The phrase might have been coined by Schiller, "whose heart, like that of the Marquis of Posa, beat for the whole of humanity, for the world, and for the coming generations." But it would hardly have occurred to Schiller that one naturally loves one's fellow-men because their lot is hard and because one is a man oneself. That is pure T.M., unsentimental and honest—modest, too, in that it precludes discussion of all and any special problems in the face of man's almost hopeless destiny.

The seventh of May, the day fixed for departure, and a Sunday, was approaching. The nearer it came, the more pressingly my father sought to assure me that he could not possibly blame me for any inadequacy in "our" address.

"God knows, you have done your best," he said, "and besides it is literally impossible to say much more in fifty-five minutes." Nevertheless he still felt misgivings in regard to the talk, and became a prey to a sort of quiet inner excitement that we had never noticed in him before. It was clear to us that he had spent himself too generously in his treatment of this cherished theme—this account of a beneficent spirit following the paths that led to light and happiness, who could do so much to heal the sickness of our age if we would only listen to him. T.M. knew that he was too deeply involved for his own peace of mind in the responsibility of identifying himself with Schiller's mission, and perhaps he heard too clearly in one of the folds of his varied being a whisper telling him that this address would be his last and for him to await the coming ordeal calmly. For days—nay, weeks—before the starting date, he was sick with travel fever, and at last, when the day came, he was standing in the hall, wearing cap and overcoat and carrying his stick and umbrella with his plaid over his arm, long before we had begun to load our baggage into the car.

The day was overcast but not cheerless, and the season (his not less than that of Rosalie in "The Black Swan") provided a variety and abundance of lovely and gracious impressions. Everything was in bloom and full of vernal brilliance, freshness, and gaiety.

At Rottweil, we stopped for luncheon, but before this we had halted on the road for a few minutes for the apéritif, which we carried with us. T.M. was in the habit of drinking a glass of vermouth before meals, and at least one of the leather-cased twin flasks that accompanied us on all our journeys was always filled with Cinzano.

We did not know Rottweil—or, at any rate, had forgotten what a delightful and enchanted place it was. Opposite our inn stood the old pharmacy, the appearance of which could persuade the traveller that he was wearing fairy boots and had strayed into a past century.

I feel that I have now reached the point at which I would like to set forth a basic principle concerning the notes I have made and propose to make. I want it to be quite clear that what I have written is not meant to impress the reader. My notes present a true account of different happenings, and my only ambition in recording them has been to mingle the important with the insignificant, the unusual with the commonplace, the unforgettable with the evanescent, just as life and time do. I hope the reader will find no reason in my text for condemning as pretentious what is merely accurate, and will not infer that I judge every episode connected with T.M., however insignificant, to be highly interesting. That is far from my purpose. But as it is not my aim to present my story in full detail, it is all the more essential that it should be accurate and properly proportioned. So let us now return to Rottweil—or, rather, back to the car.

After the midday meal, our first preoccupation was to see that my father could rest comfortably. The baggage in the back was so arranged as to be rather higher than the front seat on the right and to support the little air cushion on which our drowsy passenger rested his neck and the back of his head. We drove quickly. When we were slowed up, or even halted, by roadworks or level-crossings or by my temporary inability to overhaul a lorry, I expected on each occasion that my father would wake up with a start and want to know what was the matter. But, in point of fact, he seemed unaware of the changing tempo of our journey. He lay back, with closed eyes, in a deep and tranquil slumber. The travel fever that had plagued him before the start gave place, as soon as we were under way, to a feeling of comfortable relaxation. We knew well this change of mood. But this time it was not only the familiar and agreeable sensation of rolling through the countryside that had relaxed him but, to an even greater degree, the knowledge that he had no longer to endure the enervating suspense. . . . *It* had begun, and the secret excitement of the previous weeks had given place to the conviction that what had begun so well was bound to end happily.

The lilac was in flower in the courtyard of the Park Hotel at Stuttgart. Its white and pale-mauve heads wafted a tender perfume into our rooms. It was surprising and, in a sense, touching to notice how this scent got the better of the fumes from the exhaust of motors pouring in droves in and out of the courtyard.

A message from the Federal President informed us that he wished to meet my father, whom he did not yet know, on the very day of our arrival. So after tea T.M. went down to wait on Professor Heuss. We learned later that the meeting had taken place in the friendliest fashion and that on the following day my mother and I would have an opportunity of making the acquaintance of the head of the West German State.

We spent the evening before the opening of the Schiller Festival with a few friends and broke up early, as all of us had started early on that day and were faced with severe exertions on the morrow. As T.M. bade his friends good night, he said, "We meet tomorrow on the field of honor."

The weather on May 8th was ideal. The air, still cool, absorbed the powerful rays of the early-summer sun without becoming sultry, and the colors of United Germany—black, red, and gold—which were flying on the Park Hotel in honor of the President, billowed lazily in the gentle breeze.

We drove early to the theatre, before Professor Heuss whom an imposing crowd awaited outside the hotel. My mother was at once conducted to her seat, while I, according to my invariable custom, did not leave my father's side till it was his turn to speak. But first we were invited to visit the President, who arrived just after us, in his box. After the inevitable press photographers had filmed the two principal speakers of the day in a wild orgy of flashlights, the leading personages took their seats in the front row of the President's box.

The Festival started with music, the orchestra of the State Theatre conducted by Ferdinand Leitner giving a moving rendering of Bach's D-Major Overture. The acoustics of the house are admirable, and the finest pianissimo effects of the string instruments were audible throughout the spacious building. This performance was followed by some words of introduction and welcome from various officials, and finally my father was notified that it was time for him to go on.

From my post between the curtains on the left-hand side of the stage, I listened to "the Magician" and followed with tense interest the reactions of the invisible audience. T.M. held his hearers from the first moment. An admirable loudspeaker carried each of his words to the farthest corners of the auditorium without distorting his voice or his articulation. No creaking chairs and no coughing in the back rows indicated that anyone found it difficult to follow. But apart from these technical advantages I realized the tension of the audience, spellbound by the speaker's magic. And this result was made possible by the speaker's own enthrallment with his theme. All the emotion he had poured into his work was now being lavished on his hearers—love based on knowledge, heartfelt affection, and a deep and reverent perception, powerful enough to enable him to recreate with unembellished truth the likeness of him who had passed into the home of his immortality a hundred and fifty years before.

The Weavers of the Web—the Fates—but sway
The matter and the things of clay;
* Safe from each change that Time to Matter*
*   gives,*
Nature's blest playmate, free at will to stray
With Gods a god, amidst the fields of Day,
* The FORM, the ARCHETYPE,* serenely*
*   lives.*

* "Die Gestalt—Form, the Platonic Archetype, hovers in the Realm of the Ideal." Note by Sir Edward Bulwer-Lytton, who translated "The Ideal and the Actual Life" in his "Poems and Ballads of Schiller," 1844.

As for "our" address, I knew it by heart, word for word, and yet I listened no less intently than the strangers down below. It struck me that "the Magician" had scarcely ever spoken thus, or found so infallibly the medium in which experience and form become one, a whole, whose birth we seemed to be attending.

Enough! Or have I said too much?

It remains for me to add that in the Schiller address T.M. made a deeper impression than in any of his previous performances. After his last words, the audience rose, like one man, from their seats. People unknown to T.M., who had listened on the radio, wrote to say that they had been moved to tears. Others wrote in to admit that they had been bitterly prejudiced against the whole business from the start, not only because they had no use for the speaker himself but because they believed him quite incapable of being fair to Schiller's genius. These people asked T.M. to forgive their mistrust, of which, of course, he knew nothing. An extraordinary state of affairs! It was my father's swan song. Ought I not to have felt deep anxiety as I listened to his affecting words? Maybe, but I was happy, and happy, too, was my father when he had finished and I had received him behind the stage after his last curtain.

After having something light to eat in the restaurant, we went together to the President's box. Heuss was speaking, and T.M. followed his speech attentively and with evident interest. He sat very still. He was full of peace, the deep contentment of one who has done his best and can be sure that his best was good enough.

Social gatherings, the play, a drive to the Schiller National Museum at Marbach, and people . . . people. . . . All these filled the following days to the brim, and it is not practicable to give a detailed account of all our experiences. My diary contains a bare summary of headings covering the remainder of our Schiller journey, and I propose to limit myself to a selection from these. I shall leave out a good deal and put in a name here and there, but make no other changes.

May 8th.
Lunch with Minister President (Dr Müller) at his pretty little palace, built in 1912, in the middle of a charming parklike garden. Excellent food. Sat next Dr. Werner Schütz, Minister

of Education for Westphalia. Schütz surprised me by his accurate knowledge of T.M.'s work. Reproached me half jestingly on account of my cuts in "Faustus." Remembers from reading the "Entstehung*" that I had thrown out a whole professor, together with one of his colleagues. Knows many passages by heart, as well, especially from "Krull." Met again after twenty-six years Dr. Neinhaus, now Mayor of Heidelberg, as he was in 1929, when my father opened the dramatic festival there with his "Speech on the Theatre."

Coffee in the garden. I sat for a while by Heuss, who was in a jovial mood. The M. happy, in good form and clearly unfatigued. In the evening, "Maria Stuart." Performance goodish by present-day standards—but what does that amount to? Elisabeth (Flickenschildt) really good. Spent the interval with Heuss, and after the show went to a party he was giving in the salon of the hotel. Found that his son Ludwig Heuss, a manufacturer in Lörach, and his daughter-in-law had lunched at Rottweil at

* "Die Entstehung des Doktor Faustus, Roman eines Romans," Bermann, Fischer Verlag, 1949 (not translated into English).

the next table to us. I wonder what we talked about. Anyhow, nothing to the detriment of Heuss! Today's party full of German *Gemüt-lichkeit*. Heuss told stories. He enjoys his popularity. I disappeared early, as tomorrow morning I have to make a recording for the South German Radio on the subject "The Happy Twenties—Myth and Reality."

May 9th.
Today is really the anniversary of Schiller's death.

T.M. much pleased because the different meetings with Heuss have passed off so pleasantly. All this would have been unthinkable in the days of the Weimar Republic. But, of course, everything depends on the personality of the head of the state, in this case Uncle Heuss. Anyhow, the Ministers of Education and the senators we have met give us a feeling of confidence. The parents off to Marbach. In the afternoon, big reception by Dr. R. Pechel. The whole world present, including my radio partner of this morning, the excellent Eberle, editor of the *Stuttgarter Zeitung*. Heuss absent on duty. Otherwise, everyone present, or almost everyone.

May 10th.
Drove to Kissingen at good speed. Lovely drive. Roads scandalous in places. A good thing we have got a few days here. The M. needs a rest.

May 11th.
Weather poor. Kurgarten well kept and charming. Food moderate. Window boxes on the balconies devoid of flowers. A drab aspect, not compatible with the theory of the miraculous German economic recovery. T.M. not good at relaxing. Keeps on repeating to himself "Forward, forward," as he did on his American lecture tours. He remembers *à propos*—and laughs at the recollection—my telegram of encouragement at the beginning of one of these tours: "Let no pessimistic conjectures overcloud your lovely lectures." He always had a soft spot for Hinkel's "Gockel und Gackeleia."

May 12th.
Jankas to dinner. A good idea. They will pilot us tomorrow. The frontier of the Zone is incorrectly marked on our motor map. The road

supposed to lead to the frontier is out of use. What a state of affairs!

May 13th.

Minister Johannes R. Becher and his wife came to greet us with a great procession in Wartha. A big crowd. Flags flying in the street, but everything may have been staged. Drove on, slowly because we couldn't help it, in stately convoy. The population, which came running up from every quarter, showed real enthusiasm. Pointing to T.M., they kept saying, "That's him," with a splendid Saxon accent. There were none of Potëmkin's fake villagers. No trace of a chorus or drilled rustics. T.M. says that in 1949 things were different. Of course, there were also crowds of workers from nationalized factories, and children, many hundreds of them, if not thousands—during lesson time! Red-cheeked, merry, decently clad—many of them had come along on their own, but also school classes with their teachers. Teachers and mayors making speeches. White-uniformed traffic police rode in front of us, stopping all traffic in both directions so as not to hinder our column. Took note of the expression on faces of travellers who had been held up. They looked curious and amused, but none indignant or secretly furious. Lunch in Eisenach. How long we took covering that little bit of road! The M. as patient as ever. Very pleased with the cheerful, bustling crowds and fantastic rain of flowers. Weimar beflagged. Evening with Bechers. B.'s attachment to the M. loyal and dedicated. Town overflowing with Schiller guests, many from distant places. Pilgrims from East and West.

May 14th.

Today passed off well, too. After music—first movement of Quartet in D Minor, by Schubert —Becher was the first speaker. Short and to the point: just right. T.M. slightly handicapped by a second-rate loudspeaker. Coughing in the audience. Too few students? Still, everything went off satisfactorily. More music to finish with—first movement of Beethoven's Quartet in F Major. Becher taking enormous pains to spare T.M. and fatigue him as little as possible. Returning have found Theaterplatz with the Schiller-Goethe monument black with people listening to radio transmission and applauding loudly. People at all the windows, many with opera glasses and old-fashioned field glasses. Couldn't have been staged. Sumptuous lunch at the Elephant—no sign of Mager.* A few Russians present. The M. referred to them in his speech of thanks as "your Soviet friends." Atlantic Pacters, true to form, will doubtless represent him as having said "my Soviet friends." Never mind! Evening the "Jungfrau von Orleans." For level of performance, see "Stuttgart." Charles VII (Horst Schulze) really good. T.M. tired at last. Went home before the end.

May 15th.
While I pack and attend to the car, the M. has an honorary degree of Doctor conferred on him at the Castle. This is his seventeenth, I think. Must look it up. Professors from the Friedrich Schiller University came over in full force from Jena, with the Rector at their head. Everyone wearing robes. Professor Müller, the Germanist, spoke uncommonly well. My parents say he would have been highly appreciated *chez nous.* T.M. thanked for the honor in an extempora-

---

* The comic waiter at the Elephant in T.M.'s "The Beloved Returns" ("Lotte in Weimar").

neous speech, and also for the creation of a Thomas Mann Archive in the framework of the Berlin Academy (German Academy of Science). A tape recording was taken. Just before we left, John (Dr. Otto) insisted on having a short, pointless interview with my father, at which I was present. J. seems very unsure of himself, slightly shifty, and too good-looking, with too small hands.*

Return to Wartha, which we had left the day before yesterday. This time by autobahn. The Bechers, Jankas, and others provide a vanguard. I insist on driving at speed, as we are awaited at Göttingen. "How fast?" asks Becher. "Can you manage ninety?" I could. "That's about enough for me, too," says he. However, he set the pace, or his chauffeur did, at a hundred and twenty-five km.p.h. No doubt he hoped to take me down a peg. Baby! Laughing and perspiring, we reach the frontier together. Becher deeply moved at parting. Tears in his eyes . . .

---

* Shortly afterward, Dr. John published an account of a talk with Thomas Mann that, in all essentials, was pure invention. My father's denial, published by the U.P., followed immediately.

The customs people of the Western Zone friendly and uninquisitive.

Göttingen. Supper at the Alter Krone with the boys of the Film Aufbau Company, which made "Königliche Hoheit." We were the guests of these boys—combined ages of the three a little more than T.M.'s. (Hans Abich, the producer, away.)

May 16th.
Film Aufbau boys early at the hotel. Obligingly took all our luggage to the station. We drove there. T.M. depressed at prospect of having to change from car to train. I suddenly hesitated, wondering if it would not be better to drive to Lübeck. Decided it would be stupid, as journey by car too strenuous for parents, and besides I must hurry home. Entraining and detraining at Göttingen always a nightmare. The train usually stops too short a time. Sequence of coaches not according to plan on poster. Our porter in the wrong place, and we with him. We all had to run to the front. Parents and luggage just managed to get in, with me standing on the footboard trying to say goodbye. The

train started without warning and nearly dragged me along with it. Contrary feature of Göttingen, this, though otherwise a friendly place.

I had parted from my parents, so I now take leave of the entries in my diary. Before I saw my family again, or heard from them, the newspapers brought me more or less detailed reports about T.M.'s visit to Lübeck, including his final reconciliation with the city of his birth and his words of thanks on receiving the Freedom of the City. His speech was humorous, with an undercurrent of emotion. Anxious lest he should undertake a task beyond his strength, I had tried to dissuade him from this journey but had soon come to realize how very much it meant to him. His unalterable loyalty to his old home was all the stronger for being deeply rooted, and no separation, whether in time, space, or political views, had ever succeeded in estranging him from the familiar landscape and the breed of men among whom he grew up. Just as he had finally returned from all the world tours of his imagination in his "Faustus"

to the town of "Buddenbrooks" (for Lübeck is
the place, though he called it Kaisersaschern),
so, home at last, he stood in the Council Chamber in Lübeck, on the very spot where his father
had been elected a senator and where he had
worked and ruled. The last head of the ancient
firm of Mann, who in matters of discipline had
always been a model to his son, would surely
have appreciated with joyful wonder the recognition this deserter from business to the king-
dom of art was now enjoying, and the knowledge of this deepened and enhanced the gratitude with which T.M. received his brevet as
Citizen of Honor. Wonder, too, was not absent
from his happiness. The fact that they were
playing in his honor the overture to "Lohen-
grin" in the Stadttheater, where as a fourteen-
year-old boy he had first listened to that opera,
contained too strong an element of wish-full-
filment for him not to feel that destiny was
working a miracle for him. He himself had
given a reading for a charitable purpose, and
the proceeds of the evening's entertainment—
a substantial sum—were donated to the Hospital of the Holy Ghost, a highly respected

home for old people. My father's reading lasted an hour and a half, but neither the public nor the reader showed any signs of fatigue.

Lübeck, small but vital station on my father's journey through his year of harvest and death, no blame is yours for the tragedy of August 12th—nor can we reproach any other of the places in which he stayed and spent himself. The timepiece of his life, that delicately balanced instrument, resistant and sensitive, which kept strict time through all the assaults of danger, began to run down without warning, and no foresight, no consideration, could have halted its course.

Less than two weeks separated his visit to Lübeck from his eightieth birthday, a festival to which my father looked forward not without misgiving.

On June 7, 1954, he had written to me, saying, "Yesterday passed off peacefully amid a floral shower and a gentle rain of letters and telegrams—a mild foretaste of the foolish turmoil that next June will set going and to which I look forward with anxiety. . . ."

One can—and some certainly will—say, by

way of dissent, that no one is forced to have his birthday celebrated, that everyone is free to go away to a safe retreat and to smile from a distance at the "foolish turmoil" that might nevertheless ensue.

But T.M. had no thought of going into hiding. Whether he wished to champion a good cause or attack a bad one, to pay honor to others or to deplore their behavior, to expose himself to assault or commendation—in no case did he ride away or refuse the challenge, but only a person who misunderstood his character completely could imagine that it was vanity that induced him to spend three whole days celebrating his jubilee.

He said, while talking of his fiftieth birthday, "There are various ways of comforting oneself at one's jubilee. One hears of jubilarians disappearing into the country, bolting, so to speak, into the wilderness to escape the homage of admirers, and this attitude is sometimes honored as showing modesty and a distaste for flattery. You see, I have not done this, and I can assure you that it is not because I have an irresistible desire to be fêted and flattered but because I believe that one ought to obey the calls of life and be true to oneself and keep the feast days as they fall."

That was his belief to the end, and he remained true to himself, a man who knew anxiety, doubt, and the deepest depression, but knew no fear. I can write down those words with a clear conscience. T.M. was fearless, and fearless to an astonishing degree in a man of his nervous temperament and his easily aroused powers of imagination.

Here is an instance I shall never forget. We were flying from Sweden via Holland to England in September, 1939, shortly after the outbreak of war. My parents were sitting next to each other, and I had the seat on the other side of the aisle. My father had taken the seat by the window. My mother and I were having a conversation in English with the air hostess to which T.M. paid no attention. He probably did not hear what she told me; namely, that during the last few days Luftwaffe pilots had repeatedly forced the plane to slow down, and, flying close alongside, had stared into the windows, with the object, it appeared, of getting a shot at enemies they might see among the passengers. We were shocked to hear this piece of news, especially since it must have been as well known in Hitler's Germany as elsewhere that T.M. had been attending the International Pen Club Congress at Stockholm, and would now be on his way "home" to America. And it seemed only too probable that the Luftwaffe people would be on the lookout for him. My father was reading, and when my mother unexpectedly expressed the wish to change places with him, he raised his eyebrows in surprise and gave her his seat.

A fat man sitting on the other side had obviously heard what the air hostess said. He had slipped off the back rest of his seat and slumped sidewise, halfway to the floor. He was groaning, and beads of sweat covered his forehead. The air hostess came to attend to the poor fellow. "He must be feeling sick," said my father, "though the plane seems steady enough." In that, he was right. But even if the hostess's words had not reached T.M., he must have known that we had embarked on a very precarious and risky flight. He knew that we had given up the idea of travelling by sea because his name had been mentioned in the press as a probable ship's passenger. He also knew that a

German, who had made up to us in Malmö, had left the plane at Copenhagen. The normal way of going from Malmö to Copenhagen was by ferry, and it would not have occurred to anyone to take an air passage for such a short distance unless he had something to do or to find out during the flight in a particular plane. But my father did not seem in the slightest degree worried. He read, talked to us, and enjoyed his food.

Some days later, during a similar flight, an American engineer lost his life. This man was the brother-in-law of the New York publisher, B. W. Huebsch. He had no interest whatever for the Nazis, who nevertheless shot him dead through the window of the plane. It is probable that they got the wrong man, and were really looking for T.M. My father learned the news with sorrow and anger but without any shock to his own nerves.

All this is by the way and only designed to illustrate the absolute fearlessness of the subject of this memoir. He who was so vulnerable, so easily hurt and depressed, was completely indifferent to danger. He clung to life because he loved his work, and, as he says, during all the years that he spent down here, he had been bound by ties of affection to this green earth. But when his time came to die, he would go without fuss—and so it was.

His eightieth birthday put a great strain on his strength, his nerves, and his spiritual personality. He had constantly to find words, to improvise little speeches, and to express thanks for the overwhelming tributes these days brought him. Newspapers with congratulatory articles were piled on all the tables and chairs, but he only glanced at them casually. "Praise," he said, "is not to be recommended as a diet. It tastes sweet enough, but one soon has one's fill of it. If one considers," he continued, "for how long spiteful and malicious comments rankle in the memory, it is depressing to think how little satisfaction one gets from birthday tributes."

But this does not mean that the countless good wishes he received did not delight him. Every half hour, the postman brought bundles of telegrams, and finally the post-office officials at Kilchberg wrote to say that "the edifying activities of the telegraph staff during the week had provoked them, too, to express their felicitations." T.M. immediately thanked them, saying that he could well understand how "provoking" postal duties could become, and this made the congratulations of the post office all the more welcome.

The preliminary birthday celebration by the village community of Kilchberg, held on the fourth of June in the Conrad-Ferdinand-Meyer House, enjoyed special distinction by reason of the presence of the President of the Swiss Confederation, Dr. Max Petitpierre, who gave an address. We were assured that within the memory of man the head of the state had never visited a village to do honor to one of its inhabitants. Dr. Petitpierre, an amiable person hailing from French Switzerland, kindly gave his address in German. Only the judiciously chosen quotation from Gide with which he concluded his speech was given in French, and though he had previously spoken fluently and well, his exit into French reminded me of a fish gliding into clear water after a troublesome passage. No one speaking French as his mother tongue— how often has this been made clear to me!— can ever accustom himself to using another idiom, even in the exchanges of social life, unless he has been early transplanted to another country or has been brought up to be bilingual. To be at home in French is to have a home with which no other can compare.

My father acquired a new doctorate at the Kilchberg celebration; new, that is, not only in the sense of additional but also because it was the first of its kind to be conferred on him. Professor Dr. Karl Schmid, Rector of the Technical Higher College at Zürich, promoted our jubilarian to the grade of Doctor, *honoris causa,* of Natural Sciences, thus conferring on him his first Swiss degree, as well as the first doctorate he had ever received for distinction in anything but the humanities.

In the evening of June 5th, there was the celebration at the Schauspielhaus in Zürich, at which he derived special pleasure from the collaboration of Bruno Walter. The knowledge that his dear friend and favorite conductor, for him the greatest interpreter of music, had crossed the ocean to honor his anniversary and that now the celestial philosophy of Mozart was flowing out in a pure and powerful stream under his baton (Walter was conducting "Eine Kleine Nachtmusik") represented for him a rare and most precious birthday offering. And there was much that was uncommon in the tributes paid to him, too much for me to include in these notes. Not only Walter but my father's friend Alfred A. Knopf, the publisher, had come over expressly from the United States, and he took heartfelt interest in all the celebrations and all the speeches, though he did not understand a word of German.

For years past, T.M. had been indebted to the Zürich Schauspielhaus for many a delightful evening. And now the management paid him a special compliment by arranging a dramatic performance of a series of well-chosen episodes from his works, which continued up to the moment T.M. himself, introduced by Fritz Strich, strode onto the platform, resolved, after the examples of high oratorical skill to which his audience had listened, "to stammer out a few words." It was Strich, the eminent literary historian and Germanist, who had been the connecting link between the actors and the extracts from T.M.'s works, manipulating the transitions and creating charming and accurate vignettes for the stage, and who, in conclusion, sketched with a precise economy of words a spiritual portrait of our octogenarian. Strich was also a friend from Munich days, and his participation in the present proceedings, as well as that of Bruno Walter and Therese Giehse, may have been the principal cause of the blunder that T.M. made when returning thanks to the public. "I have always," he said to the Zürich people, "highly valued the intelligent appreciation of Munich theatre audiences. . . ." And not only the public in the theatre that evening but also countless radio listeners in Switzerland and abroad took this mistake in good part and realized that no offense was meant. After all, T.M. had lived for forty years in Munich, and if he now felt so much at home in Zürich that in a moment of present happiness, full of backward-looking recollection, his two "home towns" got confused with each other, both had the right to a certain satisfaction.

In the forenoon of June 6th, T.M. held court in our house to receive congratulations. At this ceremony, representatives of both East and West Germany were present.

All brought gifts. The monumental bust for which my father had sat for the sculptor Professor Seitz in late autumn of the previous year at our Kilchberg house was now ready, and looked gigantic in the middle of the stacked offerings. The East German delegates presented their complete edition of T.M.'s works in twelve volumes, only just published, containing practically everything he had ever printed. Meantime, Senator Dehncamp, then President of the Standing Conference of Ministers of Education, speaking on behalf of all his West German colleagues, announced to my father the creation of a Thomas Mann Fund, consisting of a sum of money to be distributed among gifted, needy, and worthy writers. The various *Länder* had contributed the sum of fifty thousand Deutschemarks, and in the distribution of this money T.M. would have the last word. That was good news for my father and deserving of his special thanks.

The children and the grandchildren were there to celebrate "the Magician's" birthday in a fit and proper manner. The Bermann Fischers gave a great reception, while friends from Switzerland—Emmie Oprecht, Richard Schweizer, and George Motschah—were hosts at a delightful supper party. Knopf invited us to a recherché luncheon. The telephone never stopped ringing, the flower vases ran short, and there was such a mass of presents that some of them have only lately been recovered from the vortex in which they had disappeared. My father took a childlike delight in his birthday presents. More than once, when I went downstairs in the small hours to get myself a glass of soda water, I found a light burning in the library. This was the room in which the presents were assembled and into which my father never came except to "borrow" or replace a book, so it was clear to me that T.M. had come down late at night to play with his toys, and had forgotten to switch off the light when he went up to bed.

Of all his presents, the ring fascinated him most. This was a gift from the family, meant to fulfill a long-cherished wish. My father loved looking at clear transparent stones, especially while he was working, and had often said how much he would like to possess a beautiful ring with a flawless stone; red, perhaps—no, preferably green. So we had gone in search of the coveted object. High-grade emeralds were hard to come by and very costly. On the other hand, the tourmaline, which we finally acquired, was within our means. It was a stone of great purity cut to suit a man's finger, while the ring it adorned looked as if it had been made for its future wearer.

My father, as I said, was delighted and could hardly wait to drive into the town with my mother to get the ring, which was a little too big for him, adjusted to his finger.

"Are you satisfied with it?" asked the jeweller. "Indeed, I am," my father assured him, "and then I find it really remarkable how a stone like this comes into being. Think of all it contains—some chlorite, for instance and . . ." The salesman blinked in bewilderment. It was clear from his expression that he had no ideas about the chlorite content of his tourmaline and that he had never considered the possibility of learning about stones from a customer. But T.M. had looked up tourmaline as soon as the stone was his own. He wanted to possess the jewel absolutely and to be able to gaze through the transparent object and become acquainted with all its qualities and components.

His birthday celebrations had not fatigued my father unduly, and I fancy that we who were present at all the festivities were at least as tired as he when all was over.

Then came the arduous business of returning thanks. As early as June 7th, cards bearing the following message and destined for the great majority of my father's well-wishers were sent to be printed:

I have much gratitude to express to many people, far too many for it to be physically possible for me to write with my own hand to thank each one individually. During these days in which I have celebrated my eightieth birthday, messages of good will have reached me from all parts of the world, showing a touching interest in my existence, my struggles, and my activities. These have taken the form of letters, telegrams, beautiful flowers, and thoughtful gifts in such an unbelievable and, even today, inestimable abundance as to make me feel at once confused, ashamed, and delighted. So now I must take advantage of this summary method of expressing my gratitude in these few printed lines, to convey to each person who has wished me well my joy in the thought that my being and doing, imper-

fect as I know them to be, and my efforts
to defend with my pen what is good and
just have won me so many friends.

In Goethe's words:

"If our coevals wish us well,
We hold a lasting proof of happiness."

I beg every recipient of this card to forget its apparent formality and believe that
it carries my personal thanks directly to
him or her.

As far as was practicable, all the cards were
signed, and often T.M. added a few lines to the
printed text. In addition, he wrote personal
letters of thanks to a great many friends. My
father spent several subsequent afternoons and
evenings and occasionally a morning in dis-
charging these duties. Nevertheless it was easy
to foresee that our task would be far from completed by the time we were due to fly to Holland, on June 30th.

After the fatigue of the Dutch tour would
come the holidays, which, this time, had most
emphatically been earned, and on the seashore
at Noordwijk there would be time for everything. Time to write letters of thanks and time

for work, which T.M. called "the active hope."
But there would also be time belonging to another dimension: sea time, a strictly private
variety, "in which 'there' is the same as 'here'
and the past the same as the present and the
future; where time is drowned in the immeas-
urable monotony of space and movement from
point to point is no longer movement—where
all is uniform and where movement is no more
movement—there is no time." I quote from the
chapter in "The Magic Mountain" entitled "A
Walk on the Seashore," to which I shall refer
again. But for the moment, of course, we had
to live in earth time—the most precisely parti-
tioned time of the flatlands, in this case called
Holland.

My father's appearances in Amsterdam and
The Hague were his contribution to the Festival
of Holland. This year, for the first time since
the war, the promoters included a German play,
"Kabale und Liebe," and, in addition, they
brought the Schiller year into their program
by inviting T.M. to speak.

The organizers of the Festival had arranged
a press conference for the morning of July 1st
at the Hotel Amstel, where, as usual, we were

staying. For more than an hour, T.M. replied to the varied questions of an army of reporters —who had, incidentally, agreed to German being the language of the proceedings. This was a striking concession, for since the days of the Occupation, the Dutch had manifested an outspoken animosity to everything German, and, their sensitivities still unhealed, they might well have resented even the sound of our language.

However, no trace of this feeling marred the atmosphere of the conference, and as for T.M.'s Schiller evening in the hall of the beautiful old University, it could not have passed off more happily and harmoniously. The audience, consisting almost exclusively of Netherlanders, followed the address so sympathetically and grasped the finest points—no less than the speaker's most elusive witticisms—so quickly and appreciatively that one might have thought homage was being paid in their mother tongue to the genius of a much loved compatriot. Whereas, instead, a German was offering homage to a German, and that German was Schiller —"the strange enthusiast," as Philip of Spain called the Marquis of Posa—whose pathos and passionate intellectuality of thought were conceivably different from the audience's way of thinking.

My father was introduced by Professor N. A. Donkersloot, and after his address was finished, the Foreign Minister, Dr. J. W. Beyen, made a short speech in the course of which he presented to the guest speaker a high Netherlands decoration in the name of the Queen. The gold-and-enamel cross of Commander of the Order of Orange-Nassau, which the Minister suspended around my father's neck, is as decorative as it is honorable. The applause of the audience kept T.M. silent for a long while. When it was hushed, he said, "Excellency, accept my heartfelt thanks for your friendly words and for the high honor that the Netherlands government has been good enough to confer on me and of which I am very proud. I should beg you to convey my thanks to Her Majesty the Queen were it not for my hope to be allowed the honor of expressing my gratitude in person.

"I can neither write nor speak your language, but nevertheless you have chosen to confer on me this splendid decoration. It is not out of vanity that I am happy to have received it but because I have a sense of the symbolic and be-

cause this order will always be for me a symbol
of your country's sympathy—a sympathy that
I reciprocate wholeheartedly. From my youth
up, I have loved and admired Holland, not only
for her culture, her literature, and her art, not
only for her friendly, intimate scenery, but also
for her truly human moral qualities, which
proved themselves so notably when a fearfully
distorted Germany, whose right to the name of
Germany I hardly recognize, inflicted on the
Netherlands and their people—in fact, on your-
selves—a load of terrible, unforgettable suffering. The heroic, unbreakable resistance with
which the people of Holland, in true union
with their Royal House, withstood this evil was
an inspiration to me and to all the world. It
was a strong consolation to those of us Germans
who at that time shunned our country because,
in place of her former features, she wore a Gor-
gon's mask. To receive honor from a land that
has endured such suffering without bowing its
knee to the tyrant is a *high* honor, and it will
give me cause for pride and satisfaction to the
end of my life."

That was the last time I heard him speak in

public. And how fresh, how unwearied, was his voice after the ordeal of his long address!

The two "days of rest" that we spent at The Hague were anything but restful. After a dinner and reception at the German Ambassador's, we went to the theatre, where we heard and greatly enjoyed two acts of Rossini's "L'Italiana in Algeri." This opera, organized by La Scala at Milan, was played in an uncommonly light-hearted and self-assured manner. It was conducted by Carlo Maria Giulini, with Italian solo singers supported by the Residentie Orchestra and the Netherlands Kamerkoor, and was probably the most successful performance of the whole Festival of Holland.

There were visits to be made and received. Foreign-press correspondents wished to meet my father, and at least some of the sights of the lovely—though, alas, seriously damaged—city had to be visited anew.

As in Amsterdam (and in every other place where the evening belonged to my father), I had inspected the building in which he was to speak at The Hague—the great church. I reported to T.M. the details of the technical installations, which I had examined, but I had to point out that the church was broader than it was long, and consequently presented difficulties to the speaker, who, if he wanted to hold the eye of the public, would have to keep moving his head (meanwhile—remembering that the microphone was immovable), turning to the left, to the front, to the right. Moreover, though there was a loudspeaker, the acoustics of the building did not seem to be first-rate. But T.M. said, "Never mind. Only, it's a pity that you won't be there. When are you flying?"

I was to take the plane at 4 P.M., so that we had time to lunch together and discuss the project in furtherance of which my father was now sending me to London.

The plan was not a new one. We had long been considering it, both in the general aspect and with a view to its practical realization. All further work on it would have to be done in consultation and collaboration with the group of persons whom T.M. hoped to win over to his idea.

The object was to induce a small number of leading intellects—writers, historians, philosophers, and persons with great names in the sphere of the humanities—to launch an appeal and a warning to the governments and peoples of the world. The doctrine we sought to inculcate was that not only was the physical continuation of human life at stake but also the honor of mankind and the moral justification for man's existence. If the guilt of men brought life on this earth to a violent end in a universal, shameful cataclysm, all the victories that man in his agelong history had gained, and the highest and purest achievements in his search for perfection through the millenniums, would go to rack and ruin.

In "Praise of Transitoriness," from "The Old and the New," my father wrote, "In the depths of my soul, I cherish the belief that, with the order 'let there be,' evoking cosmos out of chaos and the evolution of life out of inorganic being, with mankind at the highest stage of creation, a great experiment was begun. The failure of that experiment through the fault of man would be equivalent to the failure and defeat of creation itself. Whether this belief is true or not, it would be wise for men to behave as though it were true."

This was to be the motif, or one of the motifs,

of the manifesto he was planning. He did not, of course, propose to limit himself to moral arguments. Purely practical considerations had to be included, and the first concern of the group would be to employ the best, the most beautiful, the most terrifying, the most serious, the most encouraging, and the most attractive arguments that could be used in the context of the appeal—and only the best would be good enough. It was proposed to draft a short, impressive call designed not only to warn the many millions of individuals who would hear it of the catastrophic danger of the situation (they had long been warned) but to persuade them to take up an active attitude, on the ground that each one of us has a personal responsibility for the future—a matter on which the proposed manifesto would admit no compromise.

My father, of course, had no exaggerated hopes for the tangible success of such action. But even if there were no material response to an appeal and no results he could point to with satisfaction, might it not, nevertheless, exercise a quiet influence over the spirits of men? And even if it proved entirely unsuccessful, was it not good and right, and indeed necessary, that in this critical hour of man's destiny some notable representatives of human culture should let their voice be heard and take a stand for the principles they knew it was their unconditional duty to defend?

The list of the persons whom, at the start, T.M. hoped to recruit was short. In alphabetical order, they were: Pearl S. Buck (U.S.A.), William Faulkner (U.S.A.), E. M. Forster (England), Hermann Hesse (Switzerland), François Mauriac (France), Gabriela Mistral (Chile), Bertrand Russell (England), Arnold Toynbee (England), and Albert Schweitzer (Lambaréné).

In Germany, Italy, Spain, Portgual, Scandinavia, and other regions, T.M. had not yet succeeded in his search. Still, his survey was not completed, and, with the help of the first participators in his scheme, he would be able ultimately to select other candidates suitable in every respect. He felt that the Soviet Union and its allies must, in principle, remain outside the orbit of his search, as well as the Communist elements in Western countries. It was essential that, for once, a call for peace should be launched from this side of the Red frontiers, so that certain champions of co-catastrophe (or whatever the fighters in the battle against co-existence might call themselves) should have no opportunity to brand the appeal as commanded, inspired, or insinuated by the Communists or to put the word "peace" between the conventional quotation marks and so convert the concept into its opposite.

That was roughly the plan. To prepare a detailed scheme for its realization by an exchange of letters seemed too long and complicated a business. And so, as a first step, I was flying to England to enlist, if possible, the good will of the British personalities who my father hoped would join the movement.

Owing to my father's death, what I achieved or failed to achieve remained without consequence. However, let me say for the sake of good order that Lord Russell and E. M. Forster not only gladly agreed to collaborate in the scheme but made certain suggestions for its realization. Professor Toynbee declined to join. He did not wish to disparage T.M.'s project, but was of the opinion that an intellectual should not involve himself in matters in which he professionally had no competence and for which, if a crisis arose, he would not be responsible. Was it not somewhat cheap, asked the great historian, to give unsolicited advice to the persons who were in practice responsible or to try to influence them indirectly through the medium of public opinion?

That was disappointing, but we had to reckon on some failures. Moreover, we had in mind a substitute. The man we had our eye on, without possessing the powerful magnetism by virtue of which "Professor Know-All" in America attracts the spirits of men, was as prominent as the candidate who had not accepted and, like the latter, possessed the necessary world reputation.

But, in any case, it became impossible for my father to approach him or any other of the candidates from the moment the doctor ordered him to bed, on July 20th.

This July, the weather at Noordwijk was unusually fine. It often happens that the holiday season is ruined by low temperatures, continuous rain, and a stormy, inhospitable sea even in the height of summer, but this year one blue, sunshiny day followed another, and T.M. derived deep enjoyment from his visit.

He worked sitting in a chair on the seashore. Around him, chattering, noisy children built sand castles. Mothers came up to look after their brood. Fathers strode into the surf, carrying their shouting little sons. He went on writing unperturbed. The infinite expanse of the sea swallowed up, as it were, all finite noises, and in the midst of all this holiday babel T.M. devoted himself peacefully to his lonely tasks.

During the two weeks my parents spent in Noordwijk, my father wrote an introduction to "Fiorenza" for the Bremen *Weser-Kurier*. The Little Theatre of that city was preparing a revival of the play, and T.M. gladly acceded to the editor's request for a foreword. No sooner had he delivered the script than he started to work on the introduction to an anthology of "The Finest Stories of the World," which he had promised to write for the Kurt Desch Publishing Company. He worked steadily, with only a couple of interruptions from outside commitments. On July 8th, my parents attended the Dutch première in Amsterdam of the film "Königliche Hoheit," at which T.M. received an ovation from a large, but not specifically literary, audience, who manifested in the liveliest fashion their good will toward the *"Vreemdeling"* (foreigner) not only in the playhouse but also in the street.

A little later—on July 11th—he was due to be received by the Queen, in fulfillment of the wish expressed by him when returning thanks for his decoration.

The audience took place at Soestdijk, the Queen's summer residence, not far from Amsterdam. The democratic traditions of the Netherlands Royal House are well known, and the word "audience" in this context conveys no suggestion of ceremonial stiffness. The visit of my parents to Queen Juliana, though conducted according to the rules of social procedure observed at Court, passed off in an unusually unceremonious—indeed, relaxed and easy—atmosphere. For an hour and a quarter, the Queen and her guests chatted amiably together. Coffee was served—a regular form of hospitality in Holland, which is practically *de rigueur* between eleven and twelve in the forenoon. When, after about fifty minutes of conversation, the guests made a move to take their leave, the Queen declared that she was in no hurry to have them go, and so they remained with her for a while longer. Her Majesty talked about her daughters and T.M. about his grandchildren, and both revived memories of their long years of exile. Prince Bernhard, unfortunately, was absent. My parents would have been very happy to shake hands with the German Prince, who in the most difficult circumstances had won the hearts of the Netherlanders by his tact, charm, spirit, and ability, and above all by his unshakable loyalty to the land of his adoption.

On July 18th, my father first complained to my mother of a dragging pain in his left leg, which he had lately noticed and which was beginning to bother him. Occasional twinges of rheumatism were, of course, not unfamiliar to him, and he did not attach any importance to this inconvenience.

On July 20th, he came rather late to luncheon, seemingly cheerful and, indeed, in high spirits.

"The introduction is finished!" he said. "I really enjoyed doing it, especially the part about

Billy Budd. But today it was hard work walking back from the beach over the sand hills to the hotel. This stupid rheumatism . . ."

This was enough for my mother. Quite nearby, there was a clinic for cases of gout, arthritis, and similar ailments, and after lunch my mother telephoned to the doctor in charge, though T.M. did not want her to do so. He had been accustomed to use an American remedy, a sort of paste prepared by his doctor, which had helped him to get over previous attacks, but the medication was not obtainable in Noordwijk. However, he was sure that the pain would go away by itself as time went on.

Professor Mulder, the doctor, appeared and examined the leg, which he found very much swollen. This had nothing to do with rheumatism, he declared. My father was to go to bed at once and not to get up before a professor in Leyden, a celebrated specialist who was to be notified immediately, had made his diagnosis. He himself was not competent to express an expert opinion, but he would telephone the Professor for a consultation.

Shortly afterward, Professor Mulder telephoned and said to my mother, who was sitting by the patient's bed, "Your husband has a thrombosis." This was a moment in which my mother had to summon up all her strength and courage. Without betraying the slightest sign of the severe shock she had just suffered, she told my father quietly that the doctor feared an inflammation of the veins and that he might have to stay in bed for some time.

This was very depressing news for T.M., but he consoled himself with the thought that the professor from Leyden had not yet seen his leg and with the hope that after it had been examined he would be allowed to walk about a little in his room and to lie on the veranda. He could not look at the sea from his bed, and he felt that to be deprived of this pleasure for the duration of his illness would be an unreasonable hardship.

Paul Citroen had suggested coming to tea. He had made a little collection of portrait sketches of T.M. over the years and now hoped to add a new one. Should he be told not to come? My father saw no reason to put him off. After all, he wasn't really ill, and if Citroen wanted to make a drawing of him, even in bed, he did not see why he shouldn't.

Thomas Mann

20 VII. 55
Paul Citroen

"But in the meantime," he said to my mother, "give me my beautiful ring. I want to put it on and look into the stone. That will comfort me."

Citroen came. The charcoal drawing he made on this occasion turned out to be by far his most successful one. The only point to criticize in it is that the lower lip on the right side seems distorted, as though the sitter had drawn his upper lip over it or was biting it. The narrow head, with its serious expression, half-closed eyes, and inward look, represents the last likeness of my father taken before his death, and is, apart from photographs, the best we have.

During the forenoon of the twenty-first, the professor from Leyden arrived to see my father. He came into the sickroom in company with my mother, who had waited for him outside and warned him that it would be advisable, psychologically, to diagnose an inflammation of the veins. The professor complied with her request but prescribed absolute rest for the patient, who was on no account to move his leg. He added that my father had to go either to his own clinic at Leyden or to a hospital at Zürich. It was decided the latter was a feasible choice. The patient would be able to fly back to Switzerland as soon as a certain treatment, which would be applied during the coming days, had succeeded in thinning the blood sufficiently to obviate the danger of clotting. He would have to travel lying flat, and must not, in any circumstances, stand or sit up.

My parents had no hesitation in deciding on the flight. But trouble had come like a bolt from the blue. Throughout his life, T.M. had never had any difficulty with his veins. What was the source of this sudden "inflammation"? Perhaps, said my mother, in an attempt to ease her own anxiety, he had taken on too much during the past months. All those journeys—and then he had repeatedly stood for hours at a time, and possibly walking in the sand had been too much for him. That is what she said, and she longed to believe it was true. But before leaving, the professor had said something that alarmed her terribly. "Everything may be well if the thrombosis is just an uncomplicated thrombosis, and not a secondary symptom of a grave disorder, which, though it is not yet recognizable, could prove to be the source of all this trouble."

My father did not hear this and, in fact, knew nothing about it. But even the idea that he was suffering from inflammation of the veins, a by no means insignificant illness in a man of his age, did not seem to worry him. The only thing that upset him was the enforced curtailment of his holidays and the fact that he could not look at the sea from his bed. This inconvenience might have been put right before the professor's final verdict was pronounced; before his visit, the patient had counted on being allowed a certain modest freedom of movement, but now that all jolting had to be avoided, there could no longer be any question of moving his bed.

The flight took place on July 23rd, and went off smoothly.

As everyone had assured us would be so, the patient was admirably provided for in the private wing of the Zürich Cantonal Hospital, where Professor Löffler was in charge. My father's good constitution reacted exceptionally well to the treatment, and after only two weeks the doctors decided that his progress was ten days in advance of normal expectations.

I, for my part, had betaken myself to a sanatorium in Lucerne on returning from my trip to England, as I had for a long time been plagued by digestive troubles and chronic sleeplessness. But after my mother had telephoned to me from Noordwijk, although I at first accepted the theory that T.M. was suffering from inflammation of the veins, I was deeply shocked by the news of his illness, and in spite of the encouraging progress now reported, with which I kept up to date, I could not bring myself to believe in his recovery. That I should immediately wish to interrupt my cure does not need mentioning, but once again the essential thing was not to reveal to my father the full extent of my anxiety. He, moreover, urged me to carry out my purpose and complete my cure, so, for the time being, I remained where I was. After telephoning to him on the twenty-third, the day of his arrival, I took a short leave and drove to Zürich in time to visit him on the morning of the twenty-fourth.

His appearance was reassuring. He was bronzed by wind and sun, suffered no pain, and did not complain of feeling ill. He was only bitterly disappointed to have been cheated of the lovely ten days that had still remained of his holiday at Noordwijk. "I felt so *well* there," he said, "as well as . . ." He paused, and

94

finally added, "As well as I can possibly feel." He added the half sentence in a hesitating tone and without conviction, as though he had meant to say something different, something much more spirited, but at the last moment had decided on a second best. For my part, I have no doubt about what he left unsaid and why he did not say it. My father really meant that only as a child had he enjoyed the sea with such abandon as this year and that he longed for it now as he had done as a boy.

"Wind-swept wilderness, full of bitter moisture, the salty taste of which clings to our lips. We walk on and on, along the springy ground strewn with seaweed and tiny shellfish, with our ears muffled by the wind, this great, far-sweeping, soft wind, which drives through space free, untrammelled, and without malice, and fills our heads with a gentle stupor. So we wander on and on, watching the foamy tongues of the sea as it ebbs and flows, licking up to our feet. In the boiling surf, wave crashes after wave with a roar now resonant, now muffled, and races up the flat sand, over all the face of the beach, and on the banks out at sea—and this confused, universal, and gentle roar closes our ears to all the sounds of the world. Here is deep satisfaction, purposeful oblivion. . . . Close we our eyes, veiled by eternity!" I quote from "A Walk on the Seashore," which comes back once more to the memory. At the age of forty-nine, the author had nothing serious to fear from his longing for the distant sea to which he gave such eloquent expression. He was able then to say, "Love of the sea is nothing else than love of death."

Can one wonder that the sick man in the hospital in Zürich weighed his words and curbed his thoughts as he was on the point of comparing this last seaside visit with the earlier ones, perhaps the very first of all—visits that had given birth to that sentence about love and death?

For the moment—I am sure I am right about this—he was strangely moved and stirred by what he had meant to say, and it was only after I had given another turn to the conversation that he recovered his spirits. I had recently been present at a performance of the Knie Circus, and I succeeded in making my father laugh by telling him about some of the drolleries I had seen there. Generally speaking, the impression I got from my visit was favorable.

The daily telephone conversations I had with my mother after returning to Lucerne disclosed no special cause for anxiety. The examinations carried out by the doctors certainly did not justify them in concluding that he was suffering from some additional illness—or, rather, from a primary disorder of which the thrombosis was only a symptom, a secondary aspect. It was considered inadvisable to subject the patient to the strain of certain tests, especially as his condition gave no ground for suspecting unsatisfactory developments.

What reason was there for my continued anxiety? It was in vain that I told myself (among other things) that I was scared by a shadow, a misbegotten child of my own fantastic thoughts. As a matter of fact, I couldn't be sure how purely fantastic my thoughts really were, and I often wondered if, led by a sympathetic instinct, they had not found the way by secret and subterranean paths to regions where normally there is no access.

Fourteen months before, I had seen my father

die in a waking dream, the first and only one of my life, no detail of which I was able to put out of my mind.

At the time, I was in a nursing home and under the influence of a soporific, which, so far from having the desired effect on me, acted as a strong stimulant and brought me to such a condition that at two o'clock in the morning I set half the clinic in an uproar. I rushed, weeping, up and down the stairs, calling for the doctors, and was so swift and elusive in all my movements that the shocked night sister, who trailed after me, was unable to catch hold of me or to persuade me to return to my room. At last, she woke up the doctor on duty. After attending to me for some time, he sent for his colleague—not so much, I think, because he could not manage me but because he found the frenzy and despair of my hallucination so fascinating clinically that he wanted his colleague to share his experience. My father—of so much I was fearfully positive—lay dying. But, as though that were not enough, it seemed that the doctors—not those to whom I was really speaking, but some other surgeons in whose charge he was for the time being—had decided

to amputate both his legs. I had seen through
the senseless cruelty of their purpose, and as I
could not get into touch with them, I was con-
strained to beg and adjure the doctors in my
nursing home to put a stop to this unspeakable
outrage. I kept on assuring them that he was
dying of an internal rupture and that no treatment could save him. There was nothing to be
done but to stop the surgeons and avert the
senseless, hopeless crime of amputation. My
doctors promised to do everything, but they
wanted to know how I knew so much about
the case.

"I tell you I know," I repeated through my
tears, "because I found him prostrate and un-
conscious in his study, suffering from some sort
of fatal inner rupture. One only looks like that
after a rupture!"

They assured me I was mistaken; as far as
they knew, nothing at all had happened to my
father.

"Nothing happened!" I cried. "He is dying.
Where is he? Oh, where have they taken him?
It is a rupture, a deadly rupture, I swear to
you!"

My waking dream was indescribably terrible,

full of inspissated horror such as one never experiences when awake, because however much one, awake, may concentrate on the unbearable distress of a situation, one cannot help simultaneously observing things that have no relation to the miseries that torture and haunt one. But the dreamer, the nightmare dreamer, is delivered up to the horror he himself has created, and derives not the slightest relief from the neutral world, such as would be granted by feeling that it is hot or windy, that other people are present, or that the day or the night is coming to an end. The dreamer knows and perceives nothing but the horror of his dream. And at that moment all I knew and all I perceived was that he was dying. My God, a rupture! They mustn't cut his legs off—they mustn't!

As for his legs, which had carried his slender body so far and so faithfully, one of them, wrapped in an alcohol-drenched bandage, was now protected by a kind of cage, which took the weight of the bedclothes off it. It was a relief to know that an amputation was not dreamed of. Moreover, the patient was improving daily as the swelling subsided, and there was already some talk of his getting up, which meant not just a move from the bed to an arm-chair—he had already managed that more than once—but a regular little walk in the corridor.

Nevertheless I could not rid my mind of that former horror, and certain impressions and apprehensions increased my anxiety.

For instance, there was a numerical symmetry in my father's life. He was born on June 6, 1875 (a Sunday), in the middle of the year in which the century entered its last quarter; he was twenty-five when "Buddenbrooks" appeared, and in his fiftieth year (forty-nine, that is, which is seven times seven) when he completed "The Magic Mountain"; he was fifty-five when he received the Nobel Prize, and foretold his own death at the age of seventy (this prophecy, he believed, would have been fulfilled if the "Faustus" had not kept him alive); he finished building his house in Munich immediately before the outbreak of the First World War, and moved into his newly built house in California just before America entered the Second World War; he had fathered six children, a very symmetrically ordered group, who appeared, so to say, in pairs (in 1905 a girl and a year later a boy, in 1909 a boy and in 1910 a girl, in 1918 a girl and the following year a boy); and he was now eighty, and had lived just ten years longer than he had anticipated.

To this I add the following considerations. The splendid success of "Krull" had not prompted him to undertake a second volume. Instead, he had turned to the theatre—a world in which he was a stranger and that could never provide for him the milieu that every one of his stories had indicated as peculiarly his own. Then again, according to my mother, he had asked no questions about the progress of the new building being erected on the slope under our windows, nor about Nico, nor about the small additions and improvements to his beloved house, which, as he knew, were now being made, such as an added bookcase at the top landing, extra wall shelves in his study, a special stand for his birthday walking stick—the exotic cane with its delicate ivory crook. He had not asked about any of these things, and that, to my mind, was perhaps the worst and most alarming symptom.

On Monday, August 8th, I returned home

from Lucerne after a cure that, in the circumstances, had lasted long enough for my father to believe it completed.

I found the patient changed since my last visit. He had visibly lost weight—complete loss of appetite was a symptom of his otherwise quite bearable disorders—and the sunburn on his face had faded to pallor, which could, of course, be put down to lack of fresh air and exercise. As was to be expected, he asked a few questions about my cure, without any great show of interest, and then dropped the subject. But his look had suddenly become blue—a great, blue look flowing out of his gray-green eyes—and it seemed, no matter what we talked about, to contain a question that the looker would never ask and that he never put expressly even to himself, but that, I am sure, lay in the background of his mind: the question what was the significance of this illness, and would he ever leave his sickroom alive? By a final instance of numerical symmetry, his room bore the number 111.

I must not give the impression that he was despondent or inactive. He read the whole of Alfred Einstein's book on Mozart from cover to cover with deep interest. He had also begun to read Somerset Maugham's "The Summing Up," but had not got very far when his condition suddenly grew worse. He wrote letters, one of which we have kept. It was unfinished, and the address of the person to whom it was written had mysteriously disappeared, to my father's keen distress. A certain Herr Kassbaum, who had been one of T.M.'s classmates in the Katharineum at Lübeck, had recalled himself to my father's memory in writing to congratulate him on his eightieth birthday, and my father had at once resolved to write him a personal letter of thanks. He had been carrying Kassbaum's letter about with him and had begun to answer it when the letter vanished. Whether it had found its way into the pile of newspapers and letters that daily filled the wastepaper basket or had been otherwise mislaid, it was untraceable. Finally, the sick man gave up the idea of finishing his reply. "It's very unlike me to do this," he said dispiritedly. "Kassbaum—of course I remember him. What will the man think of me?"

The rest of his correspondence was handled without difficulty. An unknown patient in a neighboring room sent him some beautiful orchidlike lilies, for which he wrote to thank "Herr Konrad Kahl—Next Door." The little people, as T.M. used to call the children of his son Michael, had, one and all, written from Ischia. The letter from Frido, his favorite grandchild, with its detailed, intimate chatter, had given his fond "Granpa" special pleasure. He replied promptly, and also wrote to his old friend Erich von Kahler, to whom he thought a letter was due, and to Werner Weber, the editor of the Literary Supplement of the *Neuen Zürcher Zeitung*. My father had always had time to spare for this gifted, handsome, zealous man, and the real object of his letter, which was not in any way urgent, was to tell him about himself. The last surviving manuscript of my father's is a letter now in the possession of Lavinia Mazzucchetti, his Italian translator and the editor of the Italian edition of his collected works. In this letter, dated August 10th, he mentions some of the minor physical afflictions that worried him, but adds that he has absolutely no right to complain, as his illness is almost over.

And it was, indeed, almost over. If we

weighed the probabilities and paid no heed to the imponderables, which depressed me personally, he had every right to be in good spirits, and so had we all.

People came to visit him. There were Erich Katzenstein—a doctor friend—and Richard Schweizer, and on the tenth there arrived Dr. Martin Flinker, the editor and publisher of the lovely, unique memorial ("Hommage de la France à Thomas Mann") with which France honored the octogenarian Master.

My mother sat for nine hours every day at his bedside. While he was reading or writing, she occupied herself quietly in the sickroom. But if he wanted to talk or listen to music, she entertained him with conversation or took charge of the gramophone and long-playing records she had borrowed from a friend and brought to the clinic, and enlivened him with a short concert of favorite pieces. Short, because at this time he could stand music only in small doses. Twenty or twenty-five minutes of it was more than enough.

I tried to keep my daily visits as cheerful as possible, but I succeeded on only very rare occasions in making our patient laugh. And when

I talked to him about plans to be carried out at some future time, he seemed to be listening to something theoretically interesting that did not really concern him.

Even the news of his nomination to the Order of Merit (Civil Division), which was communicated to him at this time, moved him very little. There had been much talk about this, and people behind the scenes had repeatedly assured T.M. that this honor was to be conferred on him at the Schiller Festival at Stuttgart or, at the latest, for his birthday. The fact that it had failed to materialize had caused him no disappointment, and now the tardy news of the award, which indicated that there had, up to a short while before, been all sorts of differences of opinion in the ranks of the Knights, left him correspondingly indifferent and cool. Moreover, he had not yet received the Order itself, only the official information that it had been conferred on him.

His days were numbered. The questioning look in his gray-green eyes grew ever broader and bluer. And yet it seems that even up to the end he did not consciously expect to die. He had always felt a close attachment to and a natural sympathy for Death, though, "for the sake of kindness and love," he had weaned his mind from the obsession of mortality. Death, the dark friend, leaned over him now, but he could not recognize his features. He feared him not. And if his presence had been evident to him, he would have said so. He would have said so to my mother and bade her farewell when he was dying. That he did not do so proves the unsuspecting innocence of his surface thoughts, even if it betrays nothing of the forebodings and questionings of the deeper layers of his being.

On August 10th, he had recovered from a digestive upset, which had weakened him the day before. I found him refreshed and I felt inclined, for the first time, to make little of the fears I could not dispel and to treat them as illusions. But on the eleventh I left the clinic once more full of uneasiness. "It's not going well," I said to my brother Golo. "No, nothing special . . . No, it's the way he looks, and when I gave him a light, his hand trembled . . . his hand which never shakes." That evening, shortly before half past eight, the telephone rang, as it did so often during my father's illness.

"She isn't coming to supper," I said even before I took up the receiver. "Something must have happened." My mother's voice sounded calm. She said that he had been going to take his first little walk in the corridor that evening, but had been unable to do so. While sitting in his armchair, he had had a slight unexplainable attack of weakness, a sort of fainting fit. He was back in bed now and felt pretty well recovered. His blood pressure was normal again. But she did not want to leave him alone for the moment. She would come later, when he had gone to sleep.

Early next morning, my mother telephoned the hospital to ask how my father had passed the night. "Not a good night," said the sister. "That is why I am answering; the patient seems too weak to telephone."

My mother drove at once to the clinic. In the meanwhile, my father had collapsed. He had fallen into complete unconsciousness from which he would never have come around had not the doctors, who had been summoned immediately, recalled him to life by all the scientific means at their disposal. Even so, no progress toward recovery could, of course, be recorded. Countless injections, strengthening solutions inserted by drip technique, and two blood transfusions—these and every other treatment calculated to check the decline in his strength had failed, even temporarily, to improve his condition. Medical skill was powerless, unavailing. The most potent remedies produced no reaction. The blood pressure, which during his collapse had fallen so low as to be no longer measurable, had not risen, and the patient, though conscious, was in such a reduced condition that he could hardly comprehend what was happening to him. He knew only that this was an uncommonly disagreeable morning and remarked, though without any tone of resentment, that two doctors and a whole file of nurses seemed to be uninterruptedly busy with him. Very occasionally, as he lay there with closed eyes, he asked what they were up to. "What's happening now?" he would inquire as some new preparation was being pumped into his blood. My mother answered reassuringly, even cheerfully, that he had not eaten for so long that his stomach was empty and needed nourishment, and they were supplying this by pouring something into his veins—that was only reasonable, and it would do him good. He nodded and said, "Of course, and it isn't really unpleasant."

As I had agreed with my mother, I did not come to the clinic till about midday. I did not intend to stay longer in the sickroom than I had on the two previous days. It would have been wrong of me to increase his consciousness of these abnormal conditions by spending more time than usual at his bedside.

I was prepared for the worst, but his appearance made me catch my breath, and it was certainly not because what I saw was unfamiliar to me but because I knew and recognized the signs on this unspeakably altered face. It's the rupture, I thought. My God, the deadly rupture.

Then I touched his arm gently, saying, "It's me." He did not open his eyes but said wearily, "I can't cope with visits. I am so weak." Those were his last words to me, and I found them all the more painful because he meant thereby to excuse himself to me for not being in the mood for a talk. He thought he had to tell me how weak he felt, and I could see that he was determined to conserve his ebbing strength and to get the better of the weakness that had come over him so inexplicably—inexplicable not only to him and to us but also to the doctors, who were powerless to solve the mystery. I spoke to one of them in the passage—Dr. E., the senior physician. "Don't you see," I said, "that he is fading out? Do not go on tormenting him with injections and transfusions. Give him a sedative."

The doctor shook his head crossly. "I am fighting," he said, "and must go on fighting. It is the life of a good healthy man that's at stake. The man who was brought to us three weeks ago was not senile, nor was the man who was sitting in the armchair in there yesterday afternoon. We don't yet know what has happened to him, but we must do and continue to do what we can to save him."

I was silent but I knew in my heart that the sufferings and struggles of this day were senseless and without avail.

About four o'clock, his breathing became distressed. Golo and I, waiting in the corridor, saw the oxygen apparatus being rolled into Room

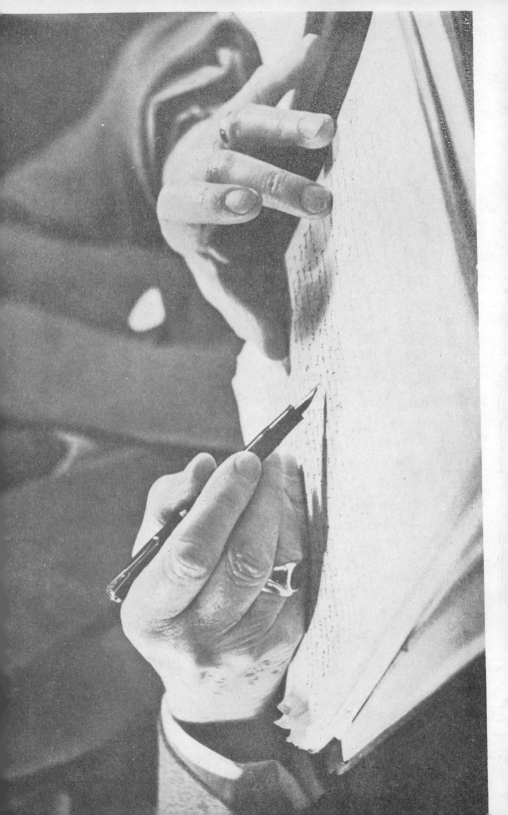

III. At half past four, the door was opened again, and a sister pushed the apparatus out into the passage.

My mother came out and said, "His breathing is easier. He has been conscious all the time."

Between five-thirty and six-thirty, Dr. E. administered morphia several times. The condition of the patient left no more room for hope, medically speaking, and so nothing was risked by thus alleviating his discomfort. On the other hand, it was not absolutely unthinkable, not beyond the bounds of possibility, that the comfort and relaxation afforded by the drug might induce his strangely recalcitrant organism to resume some part of its activities.

An hour later, my mother reported that he was sleeping. "No, don't go in," she said. "You might wake him. Before he went off, he joked with the doctor and talked to him in French and English. And then he said he wanted his glasses and only went to sleep after he had got them. Perhaps . . . it may be . . ."

Golo and I went home. My mother said there was no sense in our spending the night in the corridor. She promised to ring us as soon as there was any change, but for the time being my father was sleeping.

Arriving home, we hardly had time to take off our wet raincoats when the telephone bell rang. I heard the voice of the doctor saying, "I must inform you that your father has just died." The hands of the clock pointed to ten minutes past eight.

He had died in his sleep. The doctors had left him alone with my mother. He had not moved or altered the position of his body. Only, he had turned his head almost imperceptibly to one side and his expression had changed, as it might have done if he were dreaming. It was his "music face" that he now turned to my mother —the expression, absorbed and deeply attentive, with which he used to listen to his most familiar and beloved pieces.

"Don't you think he is breathing a little better?" asked my mother as an assistant came into the room.

The doctor leaned over him. "Just a little," he said and went out to fetch the senior physician.

It was all over.

What had happened? He had been making

such good progress; then why this collapse? And what was the reason for the failure, the total inefficacy, of the most drastic and powerful remedies?

Only the autopsy gave the solution—a solution that would probably have suggested itself as obvious in the case of any patient except one whose condition of body and mind seemed to exclude it.

Here are some extracts from Professor Löffler's findings. "I desire to report to you herewith the results of the examination, which have given us an absolutely conclusive explanation of a peculiar and complicated condition. I am glad for your sake and your family's that you authorized us to carry out this examination, and for our sake, too, because the results we arrived at show why, from the very beginning and not merely from the moment when the patient collapsed, remedial measures were condemned to failure, and make it clear that it was beyond the power of medicine to prevent a fatal issue.

"The inflammatory condition of the veins—thrombophlebitis—which declared itself apparently without any cause, was indeed, as we had assumed, on the way to being cured. But it is now clear that the thrombosis resulted from sclerosis of the arteries of the legs. In one place, the wall of the artery, which normally is in close contact with the accompanying vein, had become brittle and worn. This process had spread to the vein and, at an early stage, had caused a thrombosis. This thrombosis, however, failed to arrest the changes in the artery. Blood began to ooze increasingly through the eroded wall, until there was finally a small tear in the wall of the artery. Through this opening, no larger than a grain of rice, blood leaked into the surrounding tissue, gradually compressing the nerves and especially the sympathetic fibres, until they ceased to function. This process took some hours to develop, and was still continuing at the moment of death. The process was painless, as fortunately the area involved contained no sensory nerve fibres. One can say that what happened amounted to a block of the sympathetic nervous system. That explains why our treatment, which was essentially aimed at the sympathetic nerves, could not be effective. As to the primary disorder that brought about this result, I can say that the sclerosis of this particular artery, and of the arterial system generally, had progressed to an unusual extent and that only the cerebral arteries were unaffected. This dispensation is the happiest that persons of great age can hope for. No doubt you know the saying of Marcus Aurelius: 'It is terrible when the mind wears out before the body.' If the end had not come on Friday, grave disturbances would certainly have occurred before long in other vascular regions, possibly attended by considerable pain, so that one must say, as a doctor, that once the calamity was inevitable, it has happened as mercifully as possible."

And that was how it was: and no one, though faced by the fact that he was dying, had been able to guess how it came about.

T.M., who even during his illness looked nothing like his age, always appeared so youthfully supple, so mobile, so agile. His clear spirit was so active, so inexhaustibly fruitful, so many-sided in its interests, so energetic, and so tireless. But within his body, around his arteries, deposits of chalk had secretly accumulated that had caused the thickening of the blood, the thrombosis, and, at last, the fatal haemorrhage, the final rupture. This process could not have been arrested, and it is a wonderful example of the victory of mind over matter that there was no final degeneration in the vitality and creative power of this man and that he stood firm to the end.

If he had husbanded his strength and spared himself in the year of his harvest and death, the collapse would have followed just the same, perhaps earlier, for he felt every evasion to be a denial, and if he had withdrawn himself from active life, his spiritual surrender would almost certainly have caused him physical damage.

If one asks whether the professor's report brought consolation to us in our grief, I answer that we saw no comfort anywhere, for there was none. But the thought that grace had presided over this death as over this life was a source of thankfulness; for what would have happened if he had remained with us longer?

Would not the arteriosclerosis of which, until his last illness, he had had no symptoms have finally broken out and affected not only his body but his mind? Would he not have been confronted by the only thing he feared—the failure of his creative powers, an unthinkable horror, as he called it?

Dear, beloved Magician, grace walked with you to the end, and you went forth in tranquillity from this green earth about whose fate you have so long and lovingly distressed yourself.

For three days, your shell, your slender body, with its stern, brave, unfamiliarly waxen features, lay in the farewell chamber of the clinic. Your lovely ring was on your finger. The stone shone darkly. We buried it with you.